Awesome Inventions You Use Every Day

Exciting Entertainment Inventions

RYAN JACOBSON

LERNER PUBLICATIONS COMPANY
MINNEAPOLIS

Lerner Publications Company
A division of Lerner Publishing Group, Inc.
241 First Avenue North
Minneapolis, MN 55401 U.S.A.

Website address: www.lernerbooks.com

Library of Congress Cataloging-in-Publication Data

Jacobson, Ryan.
Exciting entertainment inventions / by Ryan Jacobson.
pages   cm. — (Awesome inventions you use every day)
Includes index.
ISBN 978–1–4677–1094–7
(library binding : alkaline paper)
ISBN 978–1–4677–1644–4 (eBook)
1. Sports—Technological innovations—Juvenile
literature. 2. Sporting goods—Technological
innovations—Juvenile literature. 3. Amusements—
Technological innovations—Juvenile literature. 4.
Inventions—Juvenile literature. I. Title.
GV745.J33 2014
688.7′6—dc23   2012047678

Manufactured in the United States of America
1 – BP – 7/15/13

CONTENTS

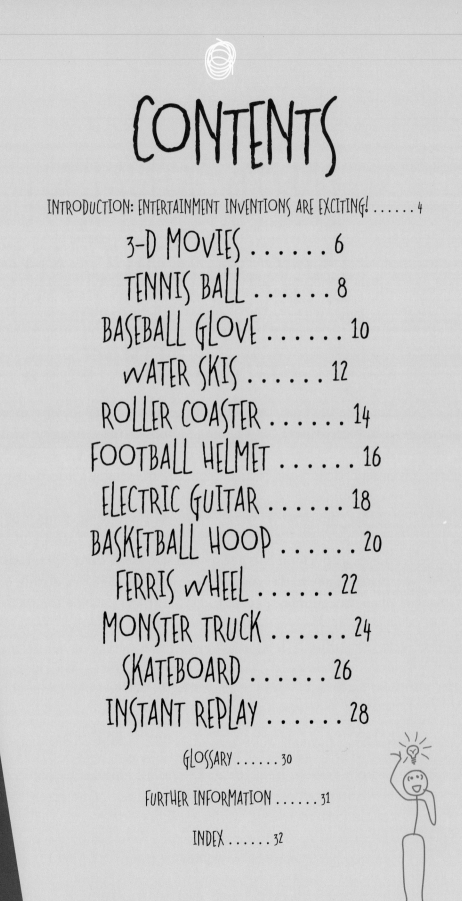

ENTERTAINMENT INVENTIONS ARE EXCITING!

You like to have fun. What do you like best? Playing sports, watching movies, or listening to music? Now imagine you couldn't do any of these things. What if they were never invented? Uh-oh. You'd probably spend your free time doing homework!

Two hundred years ago, many kids had to walk miles to reach the nearest school. When they got home, they often had to milk the cows or clean the house. But kids back then still found time to play. They had checkers, marbles, and kites. Their dolls were made out of rags or corn husks, and their building blocks and toy boats were made from wood. They didn't have many books, so storytelling was a great way to share tales. Popular games included hopscotch, knucklebones, and graces. Knucklebones was similar to a game of dice. Children rolled small animal bones and got points for how the bones landed. In graces, kids used two wooden sticks to throw and catch a large ring.

Fun and games have come a long way since then. If those kids were here today, they'd be amazed by your cool electronic games, and remote control cars. Get ready to take a look at twelve of the most awesome entertainment inventions. You'll find out why they're so amazing—and why you wouldn't want to live without them.

Checkers was a popular American pastime in the early 1900s.

Modern fun and games are often high-tech. Do you like to watch football in HD? How about playing a game of Wii tennis?

3-D MOVIES

You probably have a favorite movie. But what could make it better? Watching it in 3-D! The characters seem to pop off the screen and into your lap.

Movies were invented more than one hundred years ago. From the start, moviemakers dreamed of 3-D. They knew that people naturally see things in 3-D because each eye sees things separately. So for a movie to be 3-D, it had to send a different image to each eye.

By the early 1900s, movie audiences were using a small viewer called a stereoscope for 3-D effects. At a 3-D theater, the movie was shown in one room but on two flat screens. Two projectors—one for each screen—projected the images. People in the audience held stereoscopes in front of their eyes. The stereoscopes blended the two screens together, creating 3-D. In 1903 audiences watched a 3-D film of a train. Some viewers totally freaked out. They thought they were about to get run over!

In 1922 audiences began wearing 3-D glasses. The glasses had a green lens and a red lens. Each lens brought a different image to each eye, just like stereoscopes did. These types of glasses are still around.

Using two screens for 3-D had problems though. If the timing of one of the projectors was off, the audience got a headache. Moviemakers tried to fix this. The big solution came in 1981. Two images were printed on top of each other on the same piece of film. One projector showed both images at the same time. The 3-D glasses separated the images for each eye.

In modern times, 3-D movies are better than ever. But 3-D doesn't stop at the theater. You can buy a 3-D TV to bring the magic into your home!

TENNIS BALL

The original game of tennis has been around since ancient times. It was a lot like modern tennis. But players used their hands instead of a racket to hit the ball. They volleyed it back and forth, over a net or against a wall. The balls were made of leather or cloth, so they didn't bounce!

That changed, thanks to Charles Goodyear. The inventor spent his life working with rubber. It is naturally strong and flexible, but rubber products didn't last long in Goodyear's day. They melted when it was hot outside and froze hard in the winter. Goodyear wanted to find a solution. He tried mixing rubber with different chemicals, but nothing worked.

In 1839 Goodyear was mixing rubber with a chemical called sulfur. One day, he brought his mixture to show in a store. Customers laughed at him. Goodyear became angry and waved the rubber in the air. He accidentally threw it. Look out! It landed on a hot stove. Instead of melting, it turned into weatherproof rubber.

Goodyear began making just about anything he could think of with rubber—even dishes and hats. In the 1870s, people began making tennis balls out of rubber. The balls bounced a lot better.

Modern tennis balls are still made of rubber—but only on the outside. The inside is filled with air. The ball's rubber shell is covered with yellow felt, a type of wool. That way, the ball bounces, but not too much. Tennis balls work so well that balls for many other sports are made from rubber too!

Charles Goodyear was obsessed with rubber. His inventions led to a tennis ball that actually bounced!

The center of a modern tennis ball is air, surrounded by rubber and covered in felt.

BASEBALL GLOVE

If you play baseball, you probably know it can hurt to catch the ball. And that's with a baseball glove on. In the 1840s, during the early days of organized baseball, everyone played with bare hands. Ouch!

The first baseball gloves, made in the 1870s, weren't like modern gloves. They were thick, heavy pieces of leather with holes for the fingers. They looked a lot like modern bicycle gloves. Not many players wore them. Those who did usually wore them on both hands. And they got teased for being afraid of the ball!

Players kept hurting their hands, though. By 1900 all baseball players were wearing leather gloves. The gloves were bigger and had more padding than the earlier gloves.

In 1919 a company called Rawlings came out with a new baseball glove. It was made of thick leather and had a web of laces between the thumb and the pointer finger—much like modern baseball gloves. Players liked that they could still spread their fingers apart.

In the 1940s, somebody figured out that it was easier to catch a ball and stop a grounder if all the glove fingers were connected. So the gloves' finger pockets were laced together. They've stayed that way ever since.

Baseball gloves aren't made of tough leather anymore. Instead, most are made from lightweight, soft leather. Others are made from plastic materials. If you're not used to wearing a baseball glove, it can feel weird. But it sure beats catching a ball barehanded!

BILL DOAK (RIGHT) WAS A PROFESSIONAL BASEBALL PITCHER. In 1919 he visited the Rawlings Sporting Goods Company with an idea. He thought baseball gloves should have larger thumb pockets. He also said that a web should connect the thumb and the pointer finger. Doak's idea was a hit! It changed baseball gloves forever.

Baseball gloves let players catch a ball without hurting their hands.

WATER SKIS

Do you like to have fun in the sun? Maybe you love a trip to the beach. A swim in a lake. A ride in a boat. Perhaps you've seen someone gliding behind a boat on water skis. Maybe you've even tried it yourself. Water skiing is popular around the world. Believe it or not, it all started with two teenaged boys.

In 1922 Ralph Samuelson of Minnesota was looking for a little excitement. One day, the eighteen-year-old came up with a crazy idea: if he could ski on snow, he could ski on water too.

Ralph decided to try it. He asked his brother, Ben, for help. On June 28, Ralph tied two pieces of bent wood from a barrel to his feet. He found a line of rope and tied it to a boat. As Ben drove the boat, Ralph tried to stand straight up in the water. Wipe out!

Ralph's first attempt was a total fail. But he tried again. And again. And again. For four days, Ralph didn't give up. He tried keeping his skis flat against the water. He also tried pointing his skis slightly downward. Finally, on July 2, Ralph did something new. He leaned back and pointed his skis upward. All of a sudden, he was zooming across the water behind the boat. Ralph and Ben had done it!

The fun didn't take long to catch on. By the 1930s, water skiing was popular across the country. Soon it became popular all around the world. Water skiing was even an event in the 1972 Olympic Games! Not bad for a hobby invented by a couple of bored Minnesota boys.

Modern water skis are more durable and safer than the old wooden ones. But they are just as much fun!

Ralph Samuelson shows off his new invention in 1922.

ROLLER COASTER

If you've been to an amusement park, you've seen a roller coaster. You've probably also heard people screaming on roller coasters. But the funny thing is that as soon as the screaming people get off, they want to ride again. That's because roller coasters are a thrill!

America's first thrill ride was the Mauch Chunk Switchback Railway in Pennsylvania. The railway was built in 1827. It moved coal down from the top of a mountain. As the cars traveled down the tracks, someone got the idea to ride along. The Mauch Chunk Switchback Railway quickly became an exciting 18-mile (29-kilometer) ride up and down the mountain slope. People paid fifty cents to get pulled up the track and then to ride down it.

In 1884 LaMarcus Thompson designed a similar ride called the Gravity Pleasure Switchback Railway. It opened at Coney Island in New York and included tunnels and scenery. Riders climbed to the top of his wooden coaster and got onto a cart. The cart was given a push, and it slid down the track—with a few ups and downs along the way. It went about as fast as a person jogs. The ride was a huge success! People waited in long lines just for a chance to ride. Many consider this to be the world's first successful roller coaster. Because of his Gravity Pleasure Switchback Railway, Thompson was called the father of the American roller coaster.

Modern roller coasters have gotten much bigger and faster. Many are made out of steel. Plenty go upside down. Some have riders stand up in the cars. Others have riders dangling below the track. All are made to give riders a scary serving of fun.

Riders get an upside-down thrill on this roller coaster.

IN THE 1600S, PEOPLE IN RUSSIA GOT THEIR THRILLS ON ICE SLIDES. Riders sat on a block of ice and zoomed down a long wooden ramp covered with ice. It was very dangerous. Riders could get hurt—or even killed. But it was so much fun that the idea spread to other parts of Europe.

FOOTBALL HELMET

Football is the most popular sport in the United States. But tackling can hurt! So football players wear pads to protect their bodies. Their most important protection is the football helmet.

Football dates back to the 1870s. In 1893 college player George Barclay wore the first football helmet. It was made of leather with three heavy straps to hold it in place.

Early helmets didn't do much more than mess up the players' hair! So not all players wore them. In fact, in early football games, about half the players on the field wore helmets, while the others didn't. It was up to each player to choose whether he wanted to wear a helmet.

Finally, in the 1940s, teams started wearing plastic helmets with padding inside. Every player needed to wear one—and not just because it was safer. Tacklers sometimes rammed other players with their helmets.

In 1953 Cleveland Browns quarterback Otto Graham hurt his jaw during a game. To protect Graham's mouth in the next game, his coach Paul Brown attached a plastic bar across the front of the helmet. That bar became the first ever face mask.

In modern times, face masks are a lot bigger. Several bars cross and cover most of the face. Some players even wear plastic visors on their face masks. This protects their eyes. Plastic mouth guards protect players' teeth.

Modern helmets are made of plastic or other lightweight, tough materials. Helmets have even gone wireless! Professional quarterbacks have small speakers in each ear hole of their helmet. That way, the coaches can talk to them from the sidelines. And electronic chips in some helmets track head injuries for a safer game.

Football helmets were made of leather until the 1940s.

Otto Graham runs the ball down the field in the 1940s. He later had an injury that led to a better football helmet.

ELECTRIC GUITAR

In the early 1800s, radio and TV hadn't been invented yet. If you wanted music, you played an instrument at home or went to a concert. To actually hear the concert music, though, you had to sit pretty close to the front. If the audience was really big, this was hard to do. The only solution was to make music louder. That meant new instruments and new materials to build them with.

The first step forward came around 1890. For guitars, steel strings replaced strings made from animal guts. (Gross!) These new strings were definitely louder. And the tighter they were, the louder the sounds they could make. So guitars got bigger to stretch the strings even tighter.

By the 1920s, electricity was a part of everyday life for many Americans. In 1921 C. W. Rice and E. W. Kellogg put together the first loudspeakers. The speakers allowed music to be extra loud, perfect for two new inventions: radio and TV. Next, people wondered how to connect speakers to instruments.

In 1932 George Beauchamp designed the first successful electric guitar. The guitar's strings were connected to a speaker, which amplified the music. Other inventors, including Les Paul and Leo Fender, followed with their own designs for electric guitars.

Many people didn't like the way electric guitars sounded. They thought electric guitars would soon go away. Boy, were they wrong! Rock and roll became popular in the 1950s. The electric guitar was perfect for this kind of music, which played to huge crowds.

In modern times, electric guitars are everywhere. Can you imagine musicians like Jack White or the Black Keys' Dan Auerbach without electric guitars?

The Fender Stratocaster is one of the most popular electric guitars.

George Beauchamp designed the first successuful electric guitar (ABOVE) in 1932.

BASKETBALL HOOP

You're watching your favorite basketball team. The star player dribbles the ball down the court. He fakes going one way. He turns and spins. He stops. He pumps. He shoots. Score! And then the game stops for a few minutes. Someone has to climb a ladder and get the ball out of the basket.

That's how basketball was played more than a century ago. In 1891 Dr. James Naismith was a teacher in Springfield, Massachusetts. He wanted to invent an active game to play inside during winter. So he nailed peach baskets about 12 feet (4 meters) high on the railing of the balcony in the school gym. With a ball and a few rules—bingo—he had invented the game of basketball!

Peach baskets didn't have holes at the bottom, though. Every time somebody scored, players had to get the ball out of the basket. Eventually, peach baskets were replaced by metal hoops with nets. The hoops were like modern basketball hoops—but the nets *still* didn't have holes in them! Players still had to stop the game whenever a basket was scored.

Finally, by 1906, somebody caught on to a simple solution. The bottoms of the nets were cut off.

The modern-day basketball rim is 18 inches (46 centimeters) wide. The net is about 18 inches long. The hoop is 10 feet (3 m) off the ground, and the backboard is 6 feet (2 m) wide and about 4 feet (1 m) tall. You'd think making a basket would be easy. But even the world's best players miss about half the shots they take!

Modern hoops have metal rims with an open cloth net.

Dr. James Naismith holds two pieces of early basketball equipment—a ball and a peach basket!

FERRIS WHEEL

Not everyone loves rides that go superfast, get you dizzy, and make you want to barf. Some people like slow rides. For people like that, there's the Ferris wheel—a ride named for its inventor.

George Ferris was an engineer from Illinois. He loved railroads and bridges. Planners of the World's Fair, to be held in Chicago in 1893, wanted something big and awesome for the event. They asked for ideas. Ferris remembered a waterwheel from his childhood. It sat in a river and was much taller than he was. Buckets around the edges dipped in and out of the water as the wheel turned. The spinning wheel created power to run nearby machines.

Ferris's memory gave him an idea. He made a drawing of it on a napkin. "I'll build a monster of a wheel," he said. His friends thought he was crazy, but Ferris believed in his plan.

Ferris's "monster wheel" had thirty-six cars to sit in. It was 264 feet (80 m) high—as tall as a building with twenty-six floors. The wheel was so big that it could hold more than two thousand riders! The fair planners loved it.

Modern Ferris wheels are a lot smaller. They are usually only about 60 feet (18 m) high and hold about sixty people. Next time you're sitting at the top of one, imagine what it would have been like to be in Ferris's original invention, four times higher! How fun would that be?

The original Ferris wheel was built in Chicago in 1893.

Ferris wheels sometimes have open cars, like this one. Other cars are enclosed.

MONSTER TRUCK

Monster trucks aren't just big. They're a big deal. From TV shows to toys, monster trucks are everywhere. And it all started with a guy in Missouri.

In the mid-1970s, Bob Chandler began selling truck parts. He wanted to get attention for his new business. What's a person to do? Invent a new vehicle, of course! Chandler added big wheels to his pickup, and the monster truck was born. Before long, people started paying to see Chandler's truck. He named it Bigfoot.

By 1981 Chandler was wondering what else he could do with his truck. He brought Bigfoot to a cornfield and tried driving over some old cars. He crushed the cars with ease, so Chandler did this stunt in front of an audience. The crowd went crazy. They jumped out of their seats and ran onto the field!

Soon other drivers got in on the fun. By the mid-1980s, monster truck events included races, jumps, and other stunts. But the trucks weren't made for big jumps. Some drivers got hurt.

Chandler went back to work. By this time, monster trucks were getting bigger and stronger. Chandler made them lighter and safer—but definitely not cheaper. Modern monster trucks are so expensive to build that the engine alone costs about $35,000. Each tire costs around $1,800! You'd hate to get a flat, wouldn't you?

Racing monster trucks has grown into a billion-dollar business—and not just in the United States. Contests take place around the world!

BOB CHANDLER GAVE THE NICKNAME BIGFOOT to his famous monster truck (BELOW). Since the 1970s, Bigfoot has raced against a boat and jumped over an airplane. But it hasn't always been the same truck. There have been twenty different Bigfoot trucks over the years.

SKATEBOARD

Some things just make sense together. Peanut butter and jelly. Shoes and socks. Toothbrushes and toothpaste. And that perfect combination: board and wheels.

No one knows who invented the first one, but skateboards came on the scene about one hundred years ago. Early skateboards were made from wooden crates and the wheels of roller skates. You can thank surfers for making skateboards popular. In the 1950s, surfing ocean waves was really cool. Skateboards were a fun way to surf on land on days when the ocean didn't have big waves.

During the 1960s, skateboards became even more popular. This was because of songs like "Sidewalk Surfin'" and magazines such as *Skateboarder*. Soon companies started making better-quality skateboards with urethane wheels and fiberglass boards. That meant a smoother ride and lighter boards.

At first, skateboarders mostly showed off their wicked tricks on sidewalks and other paved surfaces. By the mid-1970s, they were looking for more challenging and exciting places to ride. They started skating in empty swimming pools! Soon some cities built skate parks to give skaters a new place to have fun. The parks even offered half-pipes, ramps, pyramids, stairs, and other obstacles to test skater skills.

Skate parks can be found in cities across the United States. You might have one near you. If you don't, check out Street League Skateboarding and other skating contests online or on TV. Street League Skateboarding has the world's top skaters competing for big money in some of the world's best arenas. No matter what, stay out of those empty swimming pools!

TONY HAWK, KNOWN AS THE BIRDMAN, is the world's most famous skater. Born in California, he became a professional skater when he was fourteen. Of his first 103 contests, Hawk won first or second place in 92 of them! Since then he has starred in books, movies, TV shows, and his own video games.

INSTANT REPLAY

You're watching a game on TV. You run to the kitchen for some more chips. All of a sudden, the coolest play in the history of sports happens—and you missed it! Luckily, you can catch the instant replay. But what if you couldn't?

Before the 1960s, that was the case. At this time, American football was dealing with a problem: too much time between plays when nothing happened. It made football boring to watch on TV. Tony Verna with the CBS television network wanted to fix this.

Football games were videotaped for television. Verna developed a way to mark the tapes with a beep before each play. That way, he could quickly rewind the tape to the beep. Then he could show the play again before the next play happened.

Verna tried out his invention on U.S. television for the first time on December 7, 1963. The football game featured Army against Navy. Late in the game, Army scored a touchdown. The play was replayed, but the TV viewers didn't understand that they were seeing an instant replay. The TV announcer had to say, "This is not live. Ladies and gentlemen, Army did not score again!"

By 1965 instant replay was more common. The ABC television network had a great idea. They began slowing down instant replays during televised baseball games. These slow-motion replays often showed whether the umpire calls were right or wrong. The idea caught on for other sports too.

In modern times, instant replay is a normal part of watching a game. So feel free to go to the kitchen for more chips whenever you want. You won't miss a thing!

Instant replay was first used on U.S. television during this Army-Navy game in 1963.

Tony Verna (LEFT) launched instant replay in 1963.

GEORGE RETZLAFF WORKED FOR A TV NETWORK

in Canada that showed hockey games. In the 1950s, he created a way to replay select plays in a game. He used it once to show a replay of a goal being scored. But Retzlaff's bosses got mad at him for it! He never tried it again.

GLOSSARY

amplify: to make a sound louder. Electric guitars connect to audio speakers to amplify their sound.

backboard: the surface behind a basketball hoop. The surface is often made of plexiglass. Basketball players sometimes make shots by bouncing the ball off the backboard.

face mask: the bars on the front of a football helmet. A face mask covers the front of a player's face to protect against injury.

ice slide: a thrill ride in which riders go down an ice-covered ramp. In earlier days, riders typically sat on chunks of ice with a straw mat for a seat.

rock and roll: a popular type of music that usually includes electric guitars and heavy drumbeats. Rock-and-roll music became popular in the 1950s when Elvis Presley hit the scene.

skate park: an area with equipment for skateboarding. Many cities across the United States have skate parks complete with ramps, stairs, tunnels, and other obstacles to offer challenging skating.

stereoscope: a small device with separate viewing holes for each eye. Held up to the face, stereoscopes allowed viewers to enjoy a 3-D effect in certain photographs and movies.

surf: to stand on a surfboard and ride atop an ocean wave

3-D: a type of movie in which characters and objects seem to pop out of the screen. The 3-D effect is created by projecting two images onto the same screen at the same time.

waterwheel: a large wheel that spins by the force of running water. As a waterwheel turns, it creates energy to make other machines work.

FURTHER INFORMATION

ESPN: Invention Hall of Fame
    http://espn.go.com/page2/s/caple/030822b.html
    Visit this page for a list of ten awesome sports inventions.

Fridell, Ron. *Sports Technology.* Minneapolis: Lerner Publications, 2009.
    Read fun details about cutting-edge sports technologies.

How 3-D Glasses Work
    http://science.howstuffworks.com/3-d-glasses.htm
    This website presents in-depth details about how 3-D works.

Kidzworld
    http://www.kidzworld.com
    At this moderated interactive website, you'll find all sorts of
    interesting sports and entertainment news.

Lynette, Rachel. *Footballs before the Store.* Mankato, MN:
    Child's World, 2012. Discover how footballs are made in this
    step-by-step guide.

Marsico, Katie. *Tremendous Technology Inventions.* Minneapolis:
    Lerner Publications, 2014. Interested in learning about other
    inventions that make our lives easier and more fun? Check out
    this title about tech inventions.

Peppas, Lynn. *Monster Trucks.* New York: Crabtree Publishing
    Company, 2012. Learn about the design behind monster
    trucks.

Sneed, Dani. *Ferris Wheel! George Ferris and His Amazing
    Invention.* Berkeley Heights, NJ: Enslow Publishers, 2008.
    Read this great introduction to Geroge Ferris, his invention,
    and his creative process.

Thomas, Isabel. *Board Sports.* Minneapolis: Lerner Publications,
    2012. Get the inside scoop on the skateboarding culture.

Tony Hawk Official Website
    http://tonyhawk.com
    Learn all about the world's most famous skateboarder.

INDEX

PHOTO ACKNOWLEDGMENTS

The images in this book are used with the permission of: Library of Congress, pp. 5 (top, LC-USZ62-71201); 11 (top right, LC-USZ62-133656); 23 (top, LC-USZ62-50927); © Sanjay Goswami/Dreamstime.com, p. 5 (bottom); © Brand X Pictures/Getty Images, p. 7 (top); © Tim Macpherson/Riser/Getty Images, p. 7 (bottom); The Granger Collection, New York, p. 9 (top); © Todd Strand/Independent Picture Service, p. 9 (bottom); © Hilary Brodey/E+/Getty Images, p. 11 (bottom); © iStockphoto.com/wdstock, p. 11 (top left), 15 (inset), 25 (top right), 27 (middle), 29 (bottom right); © iStockphoto/Thinkstock, p. 13 (top); AP Photo/Republican Eagle , p. 13 (bottom); © Paul Lemke/Dreamstime.com, p. 15; © Sports Studio Photos/Getty Images Sports/Getty Images, p. 17; © Northwestern/Collegiate Images/Getty Images, p. 17 (bottom); © Danny Martindale/FilmMagic/Getty Images, p. 19 (left); © iStockphoto.com/Christopher O Driscoll, p. 19 (right); © Audrey Baturin/Dreamstime .com, p. 21 (top); © Bettmann/CORBIS, p. 21 (bottom); © Alys Tomlinson/Photonica/Getty Images, p. 23 (bottom); AP Photo/Malcolm Clarke, p. 25 (bottom); © iStockphoto.com/Belterz, p. 25 (top left); © Dmitry Balandin/Dreamstime.com, p. (top right); © Dorling Kindersley/Getty Images, p. 27 (top); © Sianc/Dreamstime.com, p. 27 (bottom); AP AP Photo, p. 29 (top); Photo/Chris Pizzello, p. 29 (bottom left).

Front cover: © David Wall Photo/Lonely Planet Images/Getty Images.

Main body text set in Highlander ITC Std Book 13/16.
Typeface provided by International Typeface Corp.